twitturgies

personal liturgies in 140 characters or less

Gerard Kelly

INTEGRITY
MEDIA EUROPE

Integrity Media Europe
Unit 1 Hargreaves Business Park
Hargreaves Road
Eastbourne
BN23 6QW

www.integrityeurope.com
www.iworship24-7.com

ISBN 978-1-907080-32-6

Printed in the United Kingdom

Twitter as a Spiritual Discipline

2010 has been the year of Twitter. Public and personal, serious and trivial, the 140 character "tweet" has found its way into millions of lives.

When a Turkish airliner crash-landed at Schipol airport in February 2009, twitter users were the first to tell the world. 15 minutes before any news agency even knew of the crash, reports and photographs were circulating on the Internet via twitter. The speed and spread of the service took many people by surprise and for many marked the arrival of a significant new medium. Living in Amsterdam at the time, I found myself surrounded by news of the plane crash and of the role twitter had played in reporting it.

I began to reflect on this new medium and what it might mean. Could it be used, I wondered, as a means of prayer? Two things happened to me as a result. The first was a prayer that rose in my heart:

> "This day, Lord, be born in me.
> This day teach. This day heal.
> This day win, in death, surprising prizes.
> This day rise, this day rise in me."

The second was a word: *twitturgies*. Why not use Twitter as a platform for prayer – taking the prayers I was praying in any case and crafting them into personal liturgies, all the time accepting the constraints of communication in less than 140 characters? I took the Twitter question, *"What are you doing?"* and translated it as, *"What am I praying?"*

Around 1000 twitturgies later the result has been an unexpected change in my own life of prayer. Others have expressed appreciation for the prayers they have received on Twitter, but the real benefits have been in my own spirituality. By allowing my commitment to twitturgies to force upon me the regular question, *"What am I praying?"* the practice of writing twitturgies has blown a fresh breeze through my prayers. There are three key ways in which this has really helped me:

Firstly, it has empowered me to pray frequent, short prayers, peppering my day with snatched moments of prayer, rather than waiting only for the occasions when I can spend focused hours praying. I still seek out those times, but I am praying more overall by adding these shorter prayers. I don't update twitturgies at fixed times, but they are often early morning or later evening "tweets" with whatever opportunities I can find in between to use my computer or phone to pray.

Secondly, the forced constraint of 140 characters brings incredible focus to my prayers. On many occasions I have been surprised by the clarity that emerges. Twitturgies are shared with others, so they have to be interesting, accessible and easy to understand - criteria that should be perhaps applied to prayer more often. Twitter posts are the new *Haiku* and, as the Japanese have known for centuries, the constraints of form do not stifle creativity, they give it depth. The challenge of expressing heartfelt prayers in such short sentences has been a new discipline in itself.

Lastly, the practice has made me newly conscious of my own prayers and longings. My aim is that twitturgies be authentic – that is, that they genuinely reflect something I am praying about. They are prayers, not poems as such. I have to ask myself, "What do I want to say to God right at this moment?" and the questions become part of the discipline.

The result of this is that I am both a reader and a writer of twitturgies; the construction of these prayers speaks to my heart also. And because they are short and sharp, they capture very succinctly what is going on in my soul at a given moment. I archive all the prayers at *www.twitturgies.com* so they are also a kind of spiritual journal. I can look back over a day, or a series of days, and see a pattern in the prayers that have emerged. "Reading" this pattern against the events of that day or days helps me to reflect on my own spiritual journey more deeply. Twitter has become, for me, a vital part of my life of prayer.

Because it is intended to be a mobile medium, I write as often from my phone as from my laptop; it is a go-anywhere prayerbook. I have prayed "twitturgically" in between appointments, walking home from the office, during a coffee break, in a worship service, and in the last moments before sleep. Twitter is intended to be a ubiquitous service. Simple to access and quick to use, it empowers communication in places it has never been before. As such, it is remarkably suited to prayer, the other "always on" communications medium - more ancient by far, less technical, but also ubiquitous.

Twitter has become for me a kind of technological breath-prayer – a "pray without ceasing" application. In an era in which the discovery of new spiritual disciplines seems essential to the survival of faith, I have found twitturgies to be an exhilarating and worthwhile experiment, now in its third year. The twitturgies collected here are the unexpected fruits: prayers that have served their purpose in the immediacy of twitter, but just might have a longer lifespan on the page and in the lives of those who read them. I pray they will.To bring a sense of Sabbath rhythm to this one-year journey through twitturgies, I have added, for every 7th tweet, a brief reflection. Not 140 characters, in this case, but 140 words - an opportunity to pause, one day in seven, and take stock. Feel free to use these as Sunday reflections or fix another day of the week as your own 1 in 7. I pray that these thoughts, too, will be a source of blessing to you.

Gerard Kelly
February 2011
www.twitter.com/twitturgies

This Day Rise

This day, Lord, be born in me
This day teach
This day heal
This day win, in death,
surprising prizes
This day rise, this day rise in me.

———

Song

On a starless night
the chill clouds clinging
joy is singing
When fears surround
and tears abound
my hope
is found in you

wednesday

Presence

Break open God
the year as bread
Release its riches
as new wine
May its very moments
in their substance
bear your presence

—⌇⌇—

thursday

Bless the Hands

Where human ears
hear human need
bless the hands
that bless the poor
Where fears recede
and mercy moves
bless the hands
that bless the poor

friday

New

Movement stirs
on the surface of the earth
A new day dawns
a planet
ocean-deep in glory
Open my eyes God to see
and my heart
to join in

———

saturday

Perspective

When troubles
tumble in
on dismal days
remember this:
it's not the end of the world
and if it was
it would matter
even less

Glide or Slide?

Some weeks
glide to glory
Some slide
into a slump
Still God sings
"Joy, Joy, Joy"
Whatever this week
holds for you
don't lose your joy

Reflection: Slide or Glide?

To Read: Psalm 84.
This ancient song describes pilgrims on their way to Jerusalem. Even as they pass through "the valley Baca" - a dry place of bitterness - they make it a land of fresh springs, a well of joy. These are people who make more of a dent on their troubles than their troubles make on them. Something in them is strong enough that no matter what terrain they pass through, their joy remains. They are not coloured by circumstance, they re-colour their world. What will it take for you to keep your joy this coming week? What decisions can you make today to ensure that the seven days ahead become "a place of springs"? And after you have passed through the week ahead, what will you leave in your wake? Will it be the echo of unbeatable joy?

Week 2

God the Artist

God the artist
paint you into beauty
God the sculptor
shape your soul
God the gracious gardener
grow you
God your maker
make you whole

—✂—

Sunrise

Every Sunday
we remember
resurrection
Sabbath is
a point of rest
a realignment
Thank you God that
every sun that sets
in your time rises

monday

tuesday

wednesday

Weave

You take the threads of wasted lives and
weave them into grace
Each part in place
You reassemble the dismembered:
we remember who we are

—∞—

thursday

Multiply

Multiply
our resolutions God
to make the revolution
that we need
From willing hearts
forge global change

Lake

My peace
is in your presence God
I am calm
when you are close
Winds wail
and waves rise
but I will cross
this lake
with you

———

In Spite of Me

Thank you God
for your work in me
Thank you that at times
you work through me
and that when needed
you will work
in spite of me

Poustinia

May I rest, God
in the thickness
of your mercy
In the substance
of your love
may I abide
Let me not rise
from this safe place
too soon

Reflection: Poustinia

To Read: Matthew 6:5-6

In Orthodox tradition, a Poustinia is a small hut or cave, often in a private garden, set aside for prayer. A pocket-sized Cathedral, a 24-7 Prayer Room for one, the Poustinia becomes a fixed space in which to know God's presence. It's not that God isn't present elsewhere, but it helps to have a special place to seek him. Mobile phone signals are everywhere, but you need a handset to receive.

Have you experimented with such a place? Are there images or icons, sounds or smells, special settings that help you know God's presence? The writer Dylan Thomas used to ask his wife to lock him into his boat house writing room and not to let him out until he'd written something. Where can you lock yourself away to meet with God?

Week 3

Missio Dei

God the sender call you
God the sent come to you
God the spender reach you
God the spent renew you
God the Holy other wholly own you

—❦—

Loveways

More than feelings
and flutterings
love is a road we walk
a song we join
a map marked out for us
Guide us God in the
way of love

wednesday

Arrest

Arrest me God with
the beauty of your
world. Open my eyes
to see beyond
myself your glory
And to find within
myself your art

———

thursday

Jubilee

The night is long
My fears are strong
Father free me from myself
My heart grows cold
My habits hold me
Spirit set this captive free

Shalom

Freshly laundered cotton
Guitar strings
stroked with skill
Moss on old stone
God's peace comes to us
in a thousand
different gifts

—◈—

Prised

A slave set free
Land returned
to its true owner
A diamond prised
from the pawnbroker's hand
Thank you God
that you redeem

Adam

I embrace this day, God
as Adam
in a garden
you have given
In its newness I am free
May I hear you
more than fear you
today

Reflection: Adam

To read: Genesis 3:8-10

One of the roles of the book of Genesis is not to tell us how things were, but to tell us how things are. In a sense we are all Adam and Eve. Each new day or week given to us is a garden for our stewardship and care. Every circumstance God leads us through holds opportunities for fruitfulness. Every challenge we face is a challenge to obey and walk in blessing.

And every morning our eyes open, every day we take a breath, every evening we rest from our day's labours, the voice of God rings out,
"Adam, where are you?"
"Eve, are you there?"
God is looking for us. He longs to walk with us in the garden. Will you hear him and answer, or will you hide, trembling in fearful silence?

Week 4

monday

Humility

The kings of the Earth
belong to God
elephants
are infants before him
Like ladders
leaning on a tower
our tallest trees
barely touch him

———

tuesday

Found

God in whose absence
faith is found
In whose silence
love is spoken
In whose darkness
light blazes
find me now

wednesday

Restless

Chill winds
stir the trees tonight
a restless heart wakes
Is this the sound of God
sculpting
a new world?

—∿∿—

thursday

Heart

Examine my heart God
as a new year begins
Probe every part
Show every shadow
Root out all
that holds me back
from love

Clay

God who transforms
mourning into dancing
turn my anger into love
From the dry clay of
disappointment
fashion selfless joy

Future Prayer

God, we are frail
We fail
We fear and falter
Yet you call us
to be a people of the future
Guard, God of grace
the future of your people

Acts

Your words God
echo through time
unchanged
but changing everything
Trust the Father
Receive the Spirit
Tell the story of the Son

Reflection: Acts

To Read: Acts 1:6-8
After the rollercoaster events of Easter,
the disciples are anxious to know what's
next. A global empire, centred on
Jerusalem? Jesus enthroned as King?
The Romans sent packing?
None of these fit Jesus' agenda. Rather,
just three principles that will carry them
beyond their humble beginnings to become
a world-changing movement. Firstly, trust
the Father. He will decide the rise and fall
of our history; our place is to trust him and
his ultimate plan. Secondly, receive the
Spirit. Nothing will be achieved without his
power. Thirdly, tell the story of the son.
You will be "my" witnesses, Jesus says, not
"our witnesses". All three members of
the trinity are involved, vital to our faith
and life, but the story we tell is specific and
particular. It is the story of Jesus.

Week 5

Consumers

We are life consumers
Consume us
fire of God
We are comfort seekers
Great comforter
renew us
Brand us with the mark
of deep-burned love

Grounded

If God weren't good
we wouldn't know goodness
Where
God goes
good grows
What good is
God is
Ground me
in your goodness God

monday

tuesday

wednesday

Sabbath Steam

In the time it takes the kettle to boil
be with me Lord
Infuse this moment
Forge worship in me
Shape a sabbath
from this rising steam

—∿—

thursday

Home

When the house is empty
Lord be with me
each room a restful chapel
the garden
a cathedral of your peace
Father, make yourself at home

Waiting

Love led Jesus
to the cross
trust took him
to the tomb
Teach me such trust God
as I await
my resurrection
reservation

———

Safe to Fall

Into the broad
and layered grace
of God I sink
Into his great mercy
I am folded
I trust, I let go
There is no risk
in such a fall

Silent

When Heaven is silent
When you are anchored in
anxiety
unseen
unheard
Let the song of the universe
wash your ears
You are not alone

Reflection: Silence

To Read: Job 42:1-6
The book of Job is full of great speeches.
Job, his friends, his wife all talk, talk, talk
to make sense of what is happening.
But what is happening doesn't make sense.
Their huge stockpile of words makes
things foggier, not clearer.

In the end it is Job alone who understands:
what he needs to hear is not found in
words but under the words. It is when he
stops talking, finds silence and listens that
he is able, at last, to hear God's voice.
God was there all the time. But his
presence was drowned out by the words.
"I was talking about things I knew nothing
about..." Job admits.
Beneath the many words and noises you will
hear today, is God whispering to you?
Can you find silence enough to hear him?

Week 6

Materially Present

God is in the microbes
in the infinitely small
In the meanings of molecules
the purpose of each particle
Materially present
God is here

———∞———

Crowd

In this place
of crowd and clamour
God heal our isolated hearts
You who are present
even in absence
meet us here

wednesday

Evening's End

At evening's end I honour you
What has gone before
I thank you for
What lies ahead
I trust you for
my hand in yours
in the unfolding future

---

thursday

Help

My help
won't come from
the Hollywood Hills
Silicon valley
can't save me
nor can Canary Wharf
God my maker
I lift my eyes to you

Kingdom Come

In Amsterdam
as in Athens
In London as in Lille
In Berlin as in Bilbao
In Riga as in Rome
On Earth as in Heaven
let your will be done

—∽∿∿∽—

Whose?

When I forget
who I truly am
you are God
When I lose sight
of my road
you are God
God remind me
who you are and
whose I am

Continue Us

We are none of us finished .
None done.
We are half-baked
Half-built
Half-beautiful
Creator God, continue us
Craft us to completion

Reflection: Continue Us

To Read:Philippians 1:6
To his friends in Philippi - the first church
on European soil - Paul makes a huge claim.
What God has begun in you, he will
bring to completion. Acts 16 shows us the
beginnings of God's work: in Lydia, the
successful entrepreneur, in the demonised
slave girl, in the civil servant and jail
keeper. Three very different people in
three very different ways are written into
the story of God. And to these three, and
the others who have joined them, Paul says,
"This is just the beginning,
God hasn't finished yet ...
He won't give up until it's done."
God is an artist, shaping lives to be
beautiful. If you're partway on the
journey, changed perhaps a little but all too
aware that you have not changed enough,
know this: God has not finished with you yet.

Week 7

Worth It

God looks
into your heart
and sees a beauty
worth the battle
God watches
over your growth
and finds a purpose
worth the pain

———

Orphaned

Where the oppressed
hunger for hope
God let justice roll
Where the orphaned
battle bitterness
and long for love
may healing rise

wednesday

Morning Prayer

God be in my socks
in every step I take
God be in my watch
savouring each second
God be in my pulse
and in every part of me this day

———∞———

thursday

Chosen

Inspire me God
to know myself
as chosen.
Deliver me God
from thinking myself
the Messiah
Sustain me God
in surrendered service

Faith Over Fear

God help you this day
to choose faith over fear
worship over worry
service over self
If comfort comes calling
may courage answer the door

—◈—

Art

In our art be exalted, God
In invention be honoured
In making and marketing
coding and creating
in designing and
delivering be praised

sunday

Sky One

We are independent satellites
united in God's orbit
May Heaven help us
connect and communicate
and keep us from
collision

Reflection: Sky One

To Read: Revelation 5:9-14
It is a paradox of our history that
religion, with such power to bring us
together, can so crudely tear us apart.
Where people of diverse ethnicities and
backgrounds need a cause to unite around,
faith often provides the glue. Yet some of
the most violent divisions in human society
are along religious grounds.

St John's Revelation is a massive
indication that the story of Jesus is
intended to unite, not to divide. John,
whose experience is mono-cultural and
whose travels have been limited, sees a
heavenly crowd from every tribe and
tongue and nation. Perhaps he even hears
them worshipping in all their different
languages? Very much a local leader, John
predicts a global faith. Whatever else the
story of Jesus means, John understands it
as a force for unity, not fragmentation.

Week 8

In Between

Waiting for a miracle
Seeking out
God's presence
Living in the longing
May faith rise up
in these in-between
moments

———

Hidden Path

You hide the path you want for us
under the path we walk
You bury wisdom
in the places we pass
Give us, God
the determination to dig

wednesday

King of the Jungle

The kingdom of God
is a jungle of people
a garden
growing human fruit
Help me God
to know and love
the people
you have planted

———◊◊◊———

thursday

Still God

If hope at times
is hard to hold
you are still God
If dreams are dashed
desires delayed,
you are still God
Still me, God, to know you

God at Work

In my work, God
be at work
In my go-getting
may you not be forgotten
In this small room
of desks and decisions
bring my destiny to light

—◦◦◦—

Mountain Spring

The sun arrives
on time for spring duty
The mountains
unmoving, awake
May God's praises also rise
a fresh breath
in this place

Imagine Nation

If we don't ask
because we can't see
God give us more imagination
When we can't hope
because we don't dream
God set a fire in our hearts

Reflection: Imagine Nation

To Read: Ephesians 3:20
The passion that drives prayer does not come primarily from theology or doctrine, it comes from the imagination. All too often we can't pray for what we believe should happen because we can't imagine it happening. Unable to see how things could be, we cannot muster the energy required to fight for them. We simply grow used to the way things are and lose the battle against apathy.

Prayer is the gap between what is and what should be, and imagination is the bridge that helps us to cross. If you struggle to imagine what you think you should be praying for, try praying first for more imagination. Ask the Creative Spirit, who hovered over the world's first morning and fell in fire on the church's first day, to set your mind and heart ablaze.

Week 9

monday

Geneva

Lines of prestige and power
cross here
The gold of nations
buried deep
God of the poor
conquer this city again

———

tuesday

Fresh

In my praying
may I be to you fresh air, God
In my practice
may I be fresh air to others
In worship a servant
In service a worshipper

wednesday

Beginning and End

The day dawns
in hopeful faith
proclaiming
all that God will do
May it end
in faithful hope
thankful
for all he has done

—⁓—

thursday

Heart of Autumn

Don't let the sunshine
of today be wasted
on a heart of autumn, God
Don't let greyness
swallow this light
Bring spring
to my spirit too

friday

Courage

How would I know
liberation
if I never
faced the Red Sea?
What is rescue
without an army chasing me?
Give me courage God today

—∞—

saturday

Hold

Though wild winds rattle my
windows and walls
Though storms shake me
You are my foundation God
Your hold on me
is my hope

First Beat

In this newborn day's first beat
Before breath
and breakfast
talk and task
Before history takes up his pen
I dedicate an open page to you

Reflection: First Beat

To Read: Mark 1:35-39
The description of Jesus "rising early
to pray" has set a precedent to inspire
generations. Many have found, in cultures
across the world and through centuries of
change, that there is something intensely
valuable in praying first thing in the
morning. There is a clarity to praying
before other thoughts and commitments
have invaded - in Jesus' case the fact that
he was needed and had work to do.
But morning prayer is not first only in the
sense of time: it is also first in priority.
Morning prayer says, "Before all else, I want to
speak with God" and "above all
else this conversation matters to me."

Is this a commitment you can make?
Will you say, each morning this week, "I will
not take a decision/make a plan/breath
another breath until I have spoken with my
God?

Week 10

monday

tuesday

Hill Songs

On every hill around me
there are angels praising
Even when
I miss their song
night and day
come hail or sun
they praise

—–◦◦◦—–

Rain

God reign in me
Rain on me
Where you need to, reign me in
And where the song you hear
from me wears thin
let your reign, in me, begin

Ribbon

God's mercy unrolls
like a dancer's ribbon
unfurling as we watch
Just when you think
you've seen it all
more mercy
swirls around you

———

Need to Know

Today I need to know love wins
Beyond politics and power
Above scratching self
and clawing competition
God's photo finish
love wins

friday

Not All Who Wander Are lost

God's goodness
journeys with us
By day a cloud covers us
By night a fire leads us
The angel of his presence
hovers over us

———

saturday

Overcome

I do not seek
to be an overcomer
so much as to be overcome
by you God
Conquer me completely
Knock me off my feet

Cover Me

Cover me, Holy Spirit
as water the sea
deeply, fully, wholly
wave on wave
to stretch from shore to shore
Leave no part of me unsoaked

Reflection: Cover Me

To Read: Habakkuk 2:14
The image of the knowledge of God's glory covering the earth like an ocean is a wild and beautiful dream for the prophet Habakkuk. Could there be an age to come, he wonders, when God's presence will so fill the Earth?

Pentecost, years later, is a step towards just such a dream. The first disciples are overwhelmed, flooded by the Holy Spirit. The result is great joy, but empowerment too, and they begin to see their lives as a community reflecting "the knowledge of the glory of God".

Imagine your own life as dry land, suddenly flooded with an ocean-full of water. Which parts of you, now dry, would most be changed by such a soaking? Which areas are as yet untouched by God's flood? Pray, today, for the coming of God's ocean.

Week 11

monday

Inheritance

Thank you God
for the inheritance
I have in you
Vast rewards
Vaulted riches
May my eyes resist
the pull of cheaper prizes

———

tuesday

Surrender

Take this ground God
as the landing strip of heaven
Grow this garden
as your paradise on earth
Hear great creator
our heart's surrender

wednesday

Ask

God is the question
I most need to ask
God is the answer
I must find
My ask and my answer
my call and response
my God

———

thursday

Generations

Our prayers
flow into those
of generations past
With those who have blazed
a trail for us we say
God let your light
shine in our world

Coffee

In the queue for coffee
God be with me
May longing for your love
loom larger
than craving for caffeine
Amid clouds of conversation, speak

—∞—

Wise

Oil slaps and slides
towards landfall
Ash slowly clears
from our skies
Snows fall
out of season
Teach us God
to live wisely
in your world

Come Holy Spirit

Where the day is dark
and dangers hide
Where the fire in my heart has died
Where the earth cries out
for freedom's tide
Come Holy Spirit

Reflection: Come Holy Spirit

To Read: Romans 8:22-27
This is a simple, three word prayer for
almost every circumstance: Come, Holy
Spirit. To invite God's presence and
involvement in the situation, what you are
praying for is to invite, by implication,
his Kingdom to come. It is to pray for his
will to be done.

For the Apostle Paul, these are words to
use especially when you don't know what
to pray. When the challenges before you
are too painful to even bring into words.
When grief is overwhelming. When you
stand before complexities that defy
simplistic petitions.

At the graveside of a child. On the fields of
war. In the face of overwhelming cruelty
and abuse. In those moments when you
can almost hear the earth groaning.
Sometimes all you can say is, "Come Holy
Spirit". But, more often than you know, it
is enough.

Week 12

Your Weakness God

Your weakness God
makes power perfect
Your emptiness
pours out fullness
Your death in me
always leads
to resurrection

———

Thankful

Forgive my thanklessness, father
Raise me in praise
Grow me in gratitude
In the fullness
of your grace and greatness
make me grateful

wednesday

Play

I find myself
in the story of God
This drama defines me
This screenplay shapes me
May I play faithfully
the part I'm given

———✧———

thursday

Moment

I am not here for long
History and the planet
will outlive me
Even my atoms
will outlast me
God of all time redeem
the moment that is me

friday

Messiah

Bars of iron
are broken
Gates of bronze
swing open
God comes to save
Death's veil lifts
Oppression's yoke shifts
God comes to save

———

saturday

Let Kindness Rise

Let the wounds
that I have borne
bear fruit in love
May pains of the past
create in me
compassion
From brokenness
let kindness rise in me

Uncover

God's projects
outstretch mine
His perspectives wider
his purpose deeper
I don't ask God
to cover my plans
I pray
"May I uncover yours."

Reflection: Uncover

To Read: Acts 16:6-10

Not many insights are given in the Acts of
the Apostles to the means by which Paul
made his decisions and formulated his
plans. But in Acts 16 we see a remarkable
picture. Here Paul and his team are not
making plans and asking God to "cover"
them, they are uncovering the plans of
God and moving with them. By some
means or other (we are not told how) the
Spirit stops them from continuing as they
had intended. Twice the stop lights show.
Then Paul has a dream and a bold,
alternative plan unfolds.

This is the moment that the Christian faith
reached Europe - the breakthrough that was
to mean so much to world history.
It didn't come because Paul and his team
were good strategists. It came because
they were good listeners.

Week 13

monday

Unstoppable

Where we're going
total healing
How it ends
full redemption
What we're getting
resurrection
Nothing stops what God
has set in motion

—~~—

tuesday

God's Texts

Scripture is a sonnet
of love spoken over me
A symphony of life
A screenplay
of God's story
A streetmap
for my
world

wednesday

The Fight

When joy and desperation
fight for attention
God be with me
When hope and horror compete
God be the umpire
in the empire of my moods

———∾∾∾———

thursday

Steel and Iron

If there are mountains
to be climbed this week
God give me
muscles of steel
If there are valleys
to be walked through
give me
an iron will

Deo Gloria

Where is God's glory seen?
A human
fully alive
The oppressed freed
Justice done
Beauty celebrated
God, let your glory fall

—⁓—

Everlasting

Everlasting
More than bubble gum
More than love
More than the furthest edge
of an expanding cosmos
More than forever
you are everlasting

1 in 7

Sabbath =
1 day in 7
Teach me God
to set apart as sacred
1 hour in 7
1 Euro in 7
1 task in 7
1 dream in 7
1 breath in 7

Reflection: 1 in 7

To Read: Luke 13:10-17, Mark 2:27
The Old Testament is full of God's
commitment to Sabbath. From the very
beginning "1-in7" was a pillar of the
Hebrew faith. By the time of Jesus, this
had become restrictive and legalistic -
a dark and forbidding list of "don't's" with
very few "do's" for balance.

Jesus challenges this view. He heals on the
Sabbath, picks grain for his disciples, prays
for those in need. He declares the 1 in 7
principle not as God's demand, but as
God's gift to us: a rhythm of rest and
worship woven into our lives.

We set aside 1 in 7 not because only 1 in 7
is Holy. The whole earth is God's and
ours by his grace. We stop 1 in 7 to say
thank you, to remember his 24/7 presence.

Week 14

Good

Our trust
is in the goodness of God
Miracles may come
and joyous gifts fall upon us
But it is because God is good
that we thrive

—⁓—

Lectio

As I read
the words you have given
help me to reflect
on your intent
May I respond
in love and action
May I rest
in your embrace

Seeds

Ecclesia
= citizens concerned
for their city
A creative minority
A mustard seed
In time of crisis, God
make us kingdom people

———

Rest

As I set sail
on the oceans of this night
God grace my travels
In sea-deep dreams
whose waves I will not fear
God speak his rest to me

friday

Strong

God grant us courage
for all that lies ahead
With truth to be spoken
and dreams to be awoken
with curses to be broken
God make us strong

—✺—

saturday

River

Something started
the day fire fell
A river
A road
A roll call
It flows still
leading onward
Connect me God
Immerse me

Story

This is the story
we are held by
the embrace
grace grafts us into
Created free
fallen in fear
redeemed
beyond our wildest
expectation

Reflection: Story

To Read: Revelation 21:1-5
The descriptive poem that forms the
climax of John's revelatory vision foresees
God's new city: the full and final
expression of his will. This is not just the
ending of the Bible's story, it is an ending
for the human story. It is the point of
redemption and healing towards which
history is moving. It is a vision of how
things should be; of how things can be;
of how things will be.

In Genesis 1 God says, "Once upon a Time..."
and in Revelation 21 he says,
"And they all lived happily ever after."
In between, there is the tragedy of loss and the
hopeful triumph of redemption. Mourning
will be banished from this City and crying:
death vanquished and vanished. This is the
story God is writing us into. This is the
hope of the world.

Week 15

Spelling

In God's book
"receive" is spelled "give"
"success" is
"servanthood"
"Self-actualisation"
is "self-emptying"
God teach me
how to spell

—◦◦◦—

Spring

Where winter
has reigned, God
let spring break out
Where hearts are cold
ice-gripped
may your sun rise
with healing wings

wednesday

Spark

Bono's lyrics
The Dyson Airblade hand-dryer
The paintings of Makoto Fujimura
Creative
Ingenious
Beautiful
Thank you God
for the human spark

———⟞⟝———

thursday

Tuscany

These are
renaissance hills
sun-soaked, soil-rich
Abundant in fruitfulness
So may God's new birth
rise in me

Lifewide

What I pray matters
but so does what I eat
What I believe
and what I buy
How I worship
and where I work
Give me, God,
a lifewide vision

—⁓—

Drive

We travel within
the boundaries of God
The ends of the earth
are not beyond him
Drive as long as you like
you won't leave his presence

Meekonomics

The meek will inherit the earth
do business with them
The poor are blessed
seek blessing among them
God teach me the laws
of meekonomics

Reflection: Meekonomics

To Read: Matthew 5:3-10
Imagine you have been given the name
and address of someone living in your
town. You have been told a secret that
they themselves do not yet know: they
have been named in the Last Will and
Testament of a secret millionaire.
They stand to inherit a fortune.

Your job? To find them and tell them.

What would you do? I suspect that you
would drop everything to go and find them
- not for any reward, but for the sheer
pleasure of delivering such welcome news.
As you punch their address into your
satnav, you might say to your companions,
"I can't wait to see their faces."

The meek will inherit the earth, Jesus says.
The deal is sealed, in due course, by
his life given, his blood shed.

Will you tell them?

Week 16

Orphan

God embrace
the orphan in me
Welcome the widow I am
As a stranger
shelter me
Let me learn
to be your neighbour
and be loved

—〰—

Godsense

If I live as if there is no God
I am a fish that swims
as if there is no water
a tree that grows
as if there is no soil
God make me wiser

wednesday

Prague

City of culture and comedy
History and hunger
Home of reform
before reform had a name
Spirit move
in this deep place today

—~~—

thursday

Swim

Sunshine comes and goes
clouds crowd in
to put a ceiling on our feelings
The mercy of God remains
consistent as the ocean
I swim in him

friday

Outrun

No matter how long
our history goes on
we will never outrun
God's love
However far
we journey
we are never
beyond God's care

———

saturday

Search and Rescue

Guide me in the Googlesphere God
Be with me in this web
Protect me
from predators
Link me to life
As I search
may I be found by you

sunday

Bigger

God you are so much bigger
than my field of vision
That which is seen
may discourage me
That which I know to be true
stirs faith

Reflection: Bigger

To Read: Hebrews 11:1
The writer to the Hebrews makes it clear
that whatever faith is, it is not sight.
Faith might be described in terms of confidence,
of trust, of hope, of assurance - but
whichever term is used, its subject matter
is unseen.

This has two meanings for us. Firstly, that
what we see is not the full picture.
We need a wider vision, to see beyond the
seen, to take account of God's invisible
actions. Secondly, it suggests that what we
see might, at times, get in the way of this
fuller picture. God's unseen realm - the
very vista that will stir our faith - can be
obscured by our obsession with the seen.

Can you lift your eyes today, beyond the
seen, to the unseen promises of God?
It was for this that the ancients were
commended.

Week 17

monday

Life Design

As I surf the seawide surface
of Ikea
God be with me.
Cathedral of choices
Cinema of the self-constructed heart
God design my life

—⁓—

Palms

tuesday

Your limousine is a donkey
Your press corps is a children's gang
I welcome you, Jesus, as king
In your humility I honour you

wednesday

Rain

Like drops of rain
after a drought
The echo
of a distant parade
The rumbling of the rails
God's future
is breaking
into now

—◦◦◦—

thursday

Temple Prayer

Cleanse this temple too Jesus
There are moneychangers here
and thieves
at war with worship
Drive them out
Make my heart
a house of prayer

friday

Real

Every time I pray
the City of God comes closer
Every time I love
the New Jerusalem draws near
Mercy makes God's mystery
more real

—◦◦◦—

saturday

Firm

It may not be visible
It may not yet be here
For some
it may seem a mere mist
But God's future
is a firm foundation
to build on

Comforter Come

We are dry
Come Holy Spirit
We are cold, empty
hungry, thirsty, broken
Come fire, come food
Come glue, come glory
Comforter come to us

Reflection: Comforter Come

To Read: John 14:15-18
The renowned Bayeux tapestry tells the
story, among other things, of the Battle of
Hastings. In one panel king Harold is seen
poking his troops in the rear end with an
arrow, urging them into battle.
The inscription under this image is best
translated as, "Harold comforteth his troops".

To comfort, in the ancient world, was not
to make comfortable. It was to encourage,
to spur on, to urge towards battle
and perhaps death.

The comforter who comes to us brings
strength and a call to action. He comes to
piece us together, to equip us, to make us
all we should be. He sets broken bones
straight and steadies trembling knees.
"Courage," he says to us, "the battle is not
yours, but God's."

Do you hear him, stirring your heart,
stilling your fears?

Week 18

Embarking

As we cross this ocean
God be with us
Losing the shoreline
the sky wide with stars
seeking new horizons
Travelling God teach us to trust

—⟨∾⟩—

Supper

You set up a room to eat in
I set my heart for you
Wine open, bread ready
You chose to serve as waiter
I choose to wait for you

wednesday

God Friday

You came to serve
not to be served
You broke my island isolation.
Man-Friday of the cross
may this day be
God-Friday in my soul.

—◦◦◦—

thursday

God Friday 2

For me prayer
is words and thoughts
waves in air and ether
For you prayer is
wood and iron
blood and sweat; vinegar
Teach me God to pray

Stations

I travel station to station
Your burden is blistering
the fight fierce
The street smells of death
I look on
teach me to follow

—⚬⚬⚬—

37 Years

37 years I've walked this road
Still I hear my God's
unwavering cry:
"Let all that is deadly in you die
All that is godly
will be raised."

Fragrance

Beauty is found
in you God
and you are found
in beauty
Where the world releases
the fragrance
of its wonders
you are praised

Reflection: Fragrance

To Read: Romans 1:20
To understand an artist it is best to look at
her art. Creative people express themselves
in the works they create. And God has
expressed himself in all he has made:
in this planet and its people. We are
surrounded every moment with the beauty
of God.

Which means that wherever the world's
beauty is expressed, God is honoured.
All art that honours beauty, honours God.
Music that highlights harmony and touches
the human spirit speaks of God.
The unbeatable innocence of a child's smile is
the smile of God. The smell of fresh
ground coffee is the fragrance of God.

Take a look around. Do you see beauty?
Is your heart stirred with joy? Does the
goodness of life reach out to you?
That's the aftershave of God, bringing
fragrance to your world.

Week 19

monday

Cycle Prayer

The uphills are lungbreaking
the downs faithstretching
In both my God is with me
I am my best
when I can't make it alone

———

tuesday

Risen Lamb

The lamb is worthy
because the lamb is wounded
He who conquers death
carries death's scars
Wounded healer
ripped apart and risen
heal me

wednesday

Blind as I Am

When fog descends
be with me God
Though I lose my horizon
may I keep your hand
Unseen shepherd
may I know you near
Blind as I am, lead me

—∞—

thursday

Speak

I want to speak of God
as the universe
speaks of God
not in giant declarations
but in quiet
unbroken confidence
Life is
because God is

God Con Carne

Incarnation is re-creation
Word made flesh
world made fresh
Karma disarmed
curse reversed
God has a body
humanity has sanity restored

—⁓—

Sew

If you will be
the needle, God
I will be the thread
To go where you sew
To walk where you weave
May your eye
be ever on me

Matter Matters

God of matter and material
receive my praise
Rockmaker
woodshaper
soilsculptor
Particles and planets shout glory
May my soul also sing

Reflection: Matter Matters

To Read: Genesis 1:1-2

Over many centuries, spirituality has for some taken on the ethos of an escape from the material world. "Spirit" it is thought, is distinct from matter - above it, beyond it, better than it. The physical world is real and solid, but it is also flawed and dangerous. True enlightenment consists in breaking free from the material world and living fully in some other, immaterial reality.

This couldn't be further from the Bible's story. Immaterial reality, formless and empty, was what existed before God spoke. Matter is what comes next and it is after matter has been made that God says, six times, "Good."

The biblical worldview values the material world, honouring matter, loving matter, meeting God in matter. It was in the garden, not in the clouds, that God came to walk with Adam.

Week 20

Pictures at an Exhibition

Like an artist
sneaking into
his own exhibition
God visits the people
and places he loves
While we watch his works
he delights to watch us

———

Present Presence

The past
bears your footprints
The future
holds your hope
It's in the narrowness of now
I need you most
Be the presence
in my present God

wednesday

Surrender

I surrender
to God's presence
as a surfboard to a wave
As a tyre to the road
a match to flame
As a child
to love's embrace

—◇◇◇—

thursday

P S R

God, you are the paper
love is written on
You are scissors
to free us from what binds
You are a rock to build on
You win
Love always wins

Party

Graves grieve
the loves and losses
of the past
Dreams dance
with future hopes
The two meet in me
and party in
my prayers

———≈———

Emergent

We are all emerging
Out of dark
Out of fog
Out of the chaos
of discordant human cries
Into light
Into freedom
Into God
Draw us Father

Stones

Like stepping stones
across time
the movement of God proceeds
from miracle to miracle
Unless God acts
there can be
no salvation history

Reflection: Stones

To Read: Psalm 78:1-8

Imagine a long journey across a wilderness landscape. As you look forward, all you see is unmarked scrubland, harsh and flat to the horizon. But looking backwards, you see something different. At each place where you have stopped you have raised a Cairn, a pile of stones to mark your passage. Looking back, you see a line of such cairns and you know that beyond sight the line goes back to the very start of your adventure.

This is the journey of the people of God, and the function of Scripture in our lives. The stories of these texts are markers in the story of God: places we have passed through with God as guide; places where important things have happened. We guard the stories; we pass them on to remember who we are.

Week 21

Time Zone

My night falls
Your dawn breaks
I seek sleep
You are barely awake
The world speeds on
God stands watch
You and I both owe him praise

———

Aim

Give me God an even eye
a pure passion
I forget so easily
the focus I am called to
May the angle of my aim
outmanoeuvre
my amnesia

wednesday

Manifesto

I believe in consumerism
Consume me fire of God
I commit to spending
myself in love of the poor
I want to be rich
In mercy
Help me God

—⁕—

thursday

I-Thou

Give me God
a hermeneutic of humility
Confident
in knowing you speak
But not arrogant in assuming
I understand

friday

Weather Watch

Opensky days
are wide under heaven
Lowcloud days
let a ceiling seal us in
Faith's miracle calls us
to bluesky thinking
on a cloud cover day

―⌇⌇⌇―

saturday

Drawn

There is a force for good
at the centre of all things
Broken as we are
love lives
Disconnected
we are drawn
towards reunion

Dig

Where are the purposes of God?
Hidden as treasure
Buried as seeds
Lost like sons
Teach me God
to search, to dig
to watch for signs

Reflection: Dig

To Read: Matthew 13:44-46

To hear some evangelists talking, you'd think that coming to faith was the end of a long hard journey, a point of arrival for the human quest. Once a fish is caught, it seems, they quickly lose interest. This is at odds with the teachings of Jesus. Here, finding faith is the beginning of the journey. Finding the field, locating the treasure, is just the start. After comes the digging.

Throughout the gospels the kingdom of God is pictured as something to search for, to wait for, to dig for. Faith is a journey of discovery. We dig daily, turning over life's soil to find the wonders God has hidden for us. The more we dig, the more we find. God's secret riches are buried in the ground your feet will walk across today.

Week 22

War Cry

Determinism
is the enemy
of determination
Fatalism is a foe to faith
Why wrestle
when there is nothing to be won?
God, put a fighter in me

—⁓—

Exodus

The breath of God
moves the waters
The wind
makes a way
through the waves
So may the Spirit
sculpt my route to
freedom

wednesday

Scarred

Trees are the lungs of the earth
Where the cancers of our habits
have scarred our lungs
to leave a breathless planet
heal us God

———

thursday

Love Unlimited

Those who thank you God
and those who curse you
are served
by the same sun
Nor do you begrudge us grace
or limit love

Night

Though enemies
stalk me by night
by morning
my song of praise will rise
Theirs is the darkness
mine the day's new light

—❧—

Ontology

God is good
Sing it dance it
Diggit
Tweet it
Rhyme it
Repeat it
Believe it
Buy it
My liberty
My sanctuary
My ontology
God is good

Wounded

God wounded
in the weeping of Africa
God suffering
on Europe's scarred streets
God of pain
of passion and compassion
hear our prayer

Reflection: Wounded

To Read: John 20:24-29
Thomas' insistence on seeing and touching
the wounds of Jesus creates one of the most
iconic scenes of all the resurrection stories.
The doubting disciple wants to know
by touch that this event is not "virtual" or
"apparent" but real - a physical resurrection
measurable in the material world.

Jesus' invitation also bequeaths to us an
intriguing fact: the resurrected Son of God
bears the wounds of his ordeal. God is
alive but wounded, risen but wounded,
glorified but wounded. Christ's scars mean
that he will never forget the price paid.
He is wounded for us in the present
continuous tense. He suffers for us. Never
let the victory of God disguise for you
the wounds of God. All powerful he may be,
triumphant he may be, but the Lamb upon
the throne is wounded.

Week 23

Commute

Our lives flow into rivers
of traffic and trams
Arteries and veins
Our dreams crossing
colliding
Creator God speak
in this anthill city

Tide

A song of praise
rises from me
I breathe thanks
A tide of joy
flows heavenwards
as blessings rain on me
and every
drop
counts

Rumours of Glory

We bathe
in God's beauty
We swim
in his splendour
He is there in our air
our world
the womb of his wonders
Glory be born in us today

––∽∽––

Know

In a world of words
God help me
to know what I know
and to know
that I know it
I am created
I am loved
I am called to live
for others

Intimate with the Ultimate

God who fills the universe
whisper your love to me
God of the galaxies
afford me grace
God infinite and intimate
hear my heart of praise

Anchor Me

God is the reality
that earths
my expectations
his purpose the hope
that holds my attention
Ground of my being
anchor me

sunday

Return

Prairies
will praise you God
Deserts dance
Rivers will rise to sing
Rocks will rejoice
The seas salute
the return
of creation's King

Reflection: Return

To Read: Luke 19:36-40
Isaiah describes trees clapping their hands.
Jesus speaks of rocks bursting out in
spontaneous cheers. Paul writes about the
earth itself "groaning as in childbirth".
None of these phrases are meant to be
taken literally, but they are meant to be
taken seriously.

What they mean is this: even if you don't
know that the king is coming, the planet
does! Somehow, mysteriously, the creation
itself knows that God will set it free.
Christ's ultimate triumph is echoing
backwards through time, creating a stir of
anticipation in trees and rocks, causing the
very planet to tremble with excitement.

Only the religious leaders are unmoved.
"Silence this rabble," they cry. "If the rabble is
silent the rubble will sing," Jesus insists.
Don't let religion so harden your heart that
rocks have more joy than you.

Week 24

monday

Praise

To praise you God
is to breathe
To give you thanks
is to know I am alive
As a leaf responds
to the sun
so my song rises

———

Invited

tuesday

God is a party
and we've all been invited
A buffet ticket
is reserved for me
You are marked
on God's dance card
We are guests
VIP
RSVP

wednesday

Star Fuel

This hope fuels stars
there is no end to God
This wonder turns worlds
there is no end to God
This song makes me strong
God knows no end

———≈≈≈———

thursday

Forget Full

I forget that God is good
I forget I am loved
I forget my rescue
my rebuilding
the layers of grace
Heal me God
of my emotional amnesia

High Wire

If my doubts
are too deep, I drown
Where my certainties
are too strong, I stumble
Hold me God
trembling
on faith's tightrope

—✺—

A Brief History

In a temporary assembly
of borrowed molecules
journeying
from dust to dust
we live
Guide us God
in these moments
May our matter matter

Eviction Conviction

Where my heart
has been a hiding place
for pride
forgive me God
Help me in
humility
to kick it
into homelessness

Reflection: Eviction Conviction

To Read: Matthew 12:33-35
There are good things that God wants to
give you. Gifts and blessings, assurances
and joy. They are waiting on the pavement
outside your heart, in God's great delivery
truck, an army of angels ready to carry
them in.

But there are things in you that God wants
moved out. Hurts and habits, secret sins
and weaknesses. Perhaps above all, pride.
The moving out makes space for the
moving in. It can be painful. Some things
have been in place a long time. Some have
been built-in to the room. Some will leave
outlines on the walls. It's tempting to think
it's not worth the trouble. It's easy to live
with the old.

There's a delivery truck outside, full of
good things. Beside it there's a skip.
Don't be afraid to fill it.

Week 25

Good Gifts

The gifts you give us God
are great
Air and ants, coral
rain and grain
gift-wrapped, ribboned
our name on the tag
Make us grateful, God

—✳—

1st

B4 the world's 1st breath
you danced
B4 the dawn's 1st light
you rose
1st in creation
1st in resurrection
Jesus, 1stborn son
be praised

wednesday

Follow

God may I hear
and recognise
your Sprit's voice
close to me
clear to me
calling me on
Hearing, may I trust
And trusting, follow

—◦◦◦—

thursday

Gift Wrap

I wrap myself
in the one name I trust
The father who loves me
The son who found me
The Spirit who fights for me
3 in 1
my coat my armour

Crossing

A raging wall of water
left and right
I will trust
A Pharaoh's army
in my sights
I will trust
God's promises to me
my only light
I will trust

—⁓—

Rome

The story of this city
is in layers
rings in a tree
In every ring God has been present
He is present still
History is his story

Appian way

We drive away
from the city
a carpenter conquered
His words a seed
to overturn an empire
Our prayer a resonating cry
encore!

Reflection: Appian Way

To Read: 1 Corinthians 1:26-28
Rome is one of the world's most
impressive cities. Layer upon layer of
history testifies to its role in the past.
It was, in its day, the centre of the world.

The biggest impact on the life of this city
didn't come, though, through the might of
a superior empire, nor through wealth and
weapons. It came through the simple
message of a carpenter born at the edge
of the empire.

Like tree roots breaking open concrete, the
mustard seed of Jesus' life sank deep into
Roman soil. It produced fruit unheard of in
the empire of pomp and pretension.
In time, it won the heart of Caesar.

300 years to journey from the margins to
the heart of the empire, not by might, not
by power, but by the Spirit of God.

Week 26

monday

Listen

When you speak God
the earth trembles
My heart, too
is stirred
to hear
your words
May I listen well
and, listening, obey

—∾—

tuesday

Alert

Awaken my soul, God
Enliven my mind
Open my eyes
May I be alert to
your every gesture
and hear
every whispered word

wednesday

Humanic

We are breath in clay
Spirit in flesh
Mind in matter
Between angels and animals
we are meaning in meat
Creator God
inspire us this day

—ων—

thursday

Pentecost Us

Give us words, God
to cross barriers
of caste and culture
Far away or close at hand
help us understand
Pentecost our fortresses
of Babel

Maps

The treasure
of God's goodness
is buried
in everyday soil
We walk over it
work around it
often miss it
Give us maps, God
to dig for
you

⟊

The Other Side

The safe side
of life is secure
Planned
Predictable
Risks are low
adventures few
Give me courage, God
to cast my nets on the other side

Here Now

Where is God?
Some shout that
"God is nowhere"
others sing out
"God is now here."
I am learning to love
the space
that makes the difference

Reflection: Here Now

To Read: Psalm 8
Those who find the signs of God around them,
and those who find only signs of
nothing, are looking at the same evidence.
For some the very grandeur of nature
speaks of an artist's hand. For others
nature's workings need no maker.
Some who discover the vastness of an
expanding universe find it empty and
proclaim God absent. Others find it full
and declare him marvellous.

The difference is not in the evidence itself
but in how you choose to read it. If there
is no room for God in your heart, there
will be no room for him in your universe.
If he is at home in you, you will find him
everywhere.

Like evidence presented at a trial, the facts
are laid out for you without prejudice.
You are the jury.
What's your verdict?

Week 27

G Force

I can't see it
Touch it
Measure it
Contain it
Yet it holds me
In its grip I walk
I stand, I breathe
As gravity embraces me
may grace

—⟋⟍—

Rooted

You are near
Close as the air
I move through
Constant as the blood
that moves through me
Rich, mysterious
you are the soil
I'm rooted in

monday

tuesday

wednesday

Walking Backwards

Faith walks backwards
eyes on the past
Seeking roots
we find a future
Ancient stories
fuel emerging dreams
God grant us memory and hope

———— ❧ ————

thursday

Written

There is a book
that God is writing
called The History of Love
I am written in
and this is my joy
it isn't finished yet

Tune My Ear

Flowers sing
redemption's beauty
Goats bleat praise
Ducks waddle in worship
A solo leaf cries holy
Tune my ear God
to creation's choir

—⟳—

Loved

Your voice God
is like velvet
Like the creak
of a favourite door
Like morning coffee
You speak
I am known, I am loved
I am listening

Walls

Forgive me God
for dividing the world
into the impure
and the I'm pure
Tear down walls
of separation
Rebuild roads
of trust

Reflection: Walls

To Read: Ephesians 2:11-14
God is in the business of breaking down
the walls we build. Between Jew and
Gentile, male and female, rich and poor.
Between gay and straight? Between
prostitutes and preachers? Distinctions do
matter and discernment has a place, but
where we build walls to live behind, God
brings a wrecking ball. Each generation,
it seems, creates dividing issues of its own.

The test is not whether I agree with
someone or understand their choices - it is
whether I am trying to exclude them from
my world. Any attempt to build a wall in
which the people who are like me live "in
here" while others live "out there" moves in
a direction opposite to that of grace.

The church, for Paul, is a community of
grace, a place of welcome and reconciliation.
Is yours?

Week 28

monday

Everything and Nothing

Nothing that happens
changes who God is
or how he responds to me
Everything that happens
can change
who I am
and how I
respond to him

—✺—

tuesday

Creation

When technology
meets design
beauty is born
Tool and trend
together make meanings
The power of our future
the DNA of Eden

wednesday

Scent of You

Faith has a fragrance
Love lingers
Passion packs
a powerful perfume
God may I be
a scent
that you have sent
into the world

———

thursday

Sabbath

In every action
contemplation
In every strategy
sabbath
Like puddles of rain
on a grey street
may rest
arrest my progress

Isaiah 30

Quietly and confidently
I seek you God
No bling or bluster
No pride
or performance
Grant me
simplicity of soul

—⧫—

Haiku

The night falls like snow
your presence is a blanket
cradling me in peace

Ten-Fold

Thank you God
for fires that refine
Roadblocks that force
a re-think
Trials that return
a ten-fold crop

Reflection: Ten-fold

To Read: 2 Corinthians 1:3-7
Often we assume that it is through God's
blessings that we will prosper. The pattern
of the Bible suggests otherwise. It is
through trouble that God's people grow.
God guides by blocking our path.
Love shapes us in suffering. It is when we are
most tested that we triumph.

Paul suggests that comfort comes to us in
crisis and that the experience equips us to
comfort others. Not only does trouble bring
us more of God, it makes us more
godly. More trouble brings more growth,
which means that less trouble - so often
the object of our prayers - will mean
less growth.

The danger is that we will run from the
very trials God is sending for our growth.
Don't seek God only for the bouquets -
thank him for the barbed wire too.

Week 29

Empire

Where we are
half awake, God
may our heads
be lifted up
Where our empire is fake
may our idols
be torn down

—✶—

Trust

Queuing at the ATM
Teach me God
to trust in your provision
My daily bread
is not in numbers punched
but in your word to me

wednesday

Assure Me

When I need assurance
When the fires of hope burn low
Remind me, *thereforme* God
You are there
You are for me
You are for God

———

thursday

Woven

They say the devil
is in the detail
May my God be
gloriously-intricately-beautifully-finely
woven into
the details of my life

Shelter

Do not remove me
from the storm God
Do not remove
the storm from me
Shelter me rather
in the storm-breaking peace
of your presence

———⁓⁓———

Reason

When I am tempted to trust
in reason alone
remind me Father
of my reason to trust
Blind or sighted
may I hold on to you

friday

saturday

sunday

Bread

Jesus took bread
Blessed it
Broke it
Gave it
Today, God, I am taken
Blessed
Broken
I am given
May it be so

Reflection: Bread

To Read: Philippians 2:17
Christians think of bread and wine in terms
of receiving. The Eucharist is central to
our faith: Christ's body is broken and
given to us. We are on the receiving end
of love.

But elsewhere we are described as the
body of Christ. Henri Nouwen points out
an often-hidden meaning of this name.
Are we, as Christ's body, broken and given to
the world? Does our imitation of Christ
stretch to this ultimate act of self-giving?
Are we bread in the hands of God to be
broken and shared with the hungry,
wine to be poured out?

Nouwen suggests that we are and that the
act of being broken, being poured out,
being shared is the true meaning of our faith.
Paul describes his life as, "poured out as an
offering." Will yours be?

Week 30

Name in Vain

OMG
The words slip out
We claim you
We vainly name you
Yet you let us lol
btw you love us
Teach us God
to give you thnx

———

The Good in Us

Like an ancient house
undergoing renovation
a painting restored
an antique sideboard
made new
you renew
the good in us God

monday

tuesday

wednesday

Light

The light of how things were
is fading fast
The light of how things could be
isn't lit yet
Teach me God to live
in the light
of how things are

———∾∾∾———

thursday

Glory

Clouds, like cotton, catch
the sound of passing planes
Love, like lotion
holds our hurts
God, like gold, glistens
where the earth is broken

Feelings

Feelings can trip us
trap us
Turn us
Still we need to heed them
Feed them
be freed in them
God grant us joy
in our true feelings

———

Still

God moves
across our lives
like wind
on the surface of water
Without stillness
without silence
how shall we see him?

Life and Law

Your law God is life
In your design for me
is your desire
The grandest of ambitions
in the simplest of commands
"be human".

Reflection: Life and Law

To Read: Genesis 1:27-31
We see God's laws spelled out in the
Ten Commandments - in Leviticus and
Deuteronomy, in the words of Jesus,
in the admonishments of the Apostles.
But before any of these, God's first command
to us was "be". To *be* fruitful, to multiply,
to steward the garden given to us.
God's deepest laws are creational and our
deepest duty is to be human.

This is the foundation on which all other
laws rest. The Commandments shape and
preserve our humanity until the redeemer
can come. Jesus speaks life into
our humanity and breaks the power of that
which has distorted it. The apostles help
the new communities of redeemed
humanity to live in the freedom Christ
has brought them.

All the time, God's original intention
stands: "be". What ambitions does he have
for your humanity?

Week 31

Original

God give me hindsight
beyond sin to see
the originality of blessing
God give me foresight
beyond judgement to grasp
the finality of bliss

———∽∽∽———

Hear, Now

We mine the earth
for gold and jewels
We probe deep space
for knowledge
But wisdom is found
in the hear and now
God's words
working in our lives

monday
tuesday

wednesday

Love Wins

At the centre
of the universe
there beats a heart
of mercy
In the deepest places
grace abides
When all else falls
love will win

—◦◦◦—

thursday

Iran

Protest
is the twin of prayer
In both we cry for change
we break the silence
we give our hunger voice
In both our dreams
wear boots

friday

Altitude

The landscape decides
when there are hills to climb
not my plans
nor my dreams
God give me the attitude
for the altitude I meet

———

saturday

You-nique

My DNA
is 98% monkey
My reactions
are as common as a cold
My face is a blur in the crowd
But there is no other me
God my maker
thank you

Tied

This is freedom
not to be loosed
from every tie
but to be held
by a heart
that beats for me
Bind me God
to this freedom

Reflection: Tied

To Read: Hosea 11:1-4

Freedom, in God's story, does not consist in being liberated from relational responsibility, but of being freed in relationship. The more modern belief that liberation means freedom from all ties is death to us. God's offer of freedom is covenantal: the freedom of a relationship founded on faithful love.

The Hebrews are freed from the cruelty of Pharaoh's mastery. The yoke of slavery is lifted from them. They are offered instead a new master. One who loves them and wants the best for them. One who will replace the whips of servitude with the cords of love. But a master he is and commitment is required. Freedom without relationship is a dangerous illusion. We are at our best not in independence but, interdependence. What might the freedom of covenant mean to you today?

Week 32

monday

People of Colour

Our colours carry
the complexity of God
Our diversity defines him
The polychrome splendour
pouring from creation
paints
the maker's magnificence

———

Prayers Rise

tuesday

Chimneys scratch
the evening sky
and send their smoke to heaven
So may my prayers rise
at this day's end
God hear my heart

wednesday

To Boldly Go

Where we are oceans apart
may God give us
the curiosity of Columbus
If we are on different planets
grant us God
the boldness of James Kirk

---

thursday

Eye Test

Test the eyes
of my soul God
If I am shortsighted
stretch me
If I am blind
heal me
Where I harbour darkness
send your light

Speakeasy

Language is a bouquet
held out to those we love
and barbed wire
between us
and those we don't
Give us, God, the gift
of speaking in tongues

—⁓—

Perfect Parent

The wings
of the dove of love
ever cover you
The songs
of the strong son of God
surround you
May your maker
perfect parent
be your peace

No Loose Change

What changes
does God ask of us?
What sacrifices
would he have us make?
Only those
that perfect love in us
Only that
by which we shine

Reflection: No Loose Change

To Read: Ephesians 4:14-16

An accusation often levelled at governments is that they pursue change for its own sake. A new administration takes office and suddenly plans are in place for an extreme make-over of a particular public service or a wholesale revision of some long-held law. The problem, critics will claim, is that the changes are often cosmetic and ideologically driven. They don't really fix anything.

This isn't how God works. There is no loose change in his economy - no transformation demanded just for the sake of it. The changes God asks for have one goal: to bring us to maturity. God loves us as we are, but loves us far too much to leave us this way. He will work with us and in us until we are transformed into the likeness of Christ.

Week 33

Clouds

Every cloud
has a sacred lining
The sparkle of the spirit
nestles in the everyday
Give me eyes to see God
and a heart and words to praise

—◦◦◦—

Again

A fresh start
A new page
A return
to innocence
Debts cancelled
errors undone
Being born again
is more than
just religion

wednesday

Heavy With Hope

Show me God
where impossible things
are breaking through in your name
Lead me to pregnant places
where today is heavy
with tomorrow's hope

———

thursday

Tunnels

God's ways
are not only
higher than ours
but deeper too
He tunnels under us
What is real
may not always
be explained
by what is seen

Ex

God make me an ex-believer
created *ex nihilio*
freed by your exodus
sustained in exile
burned by extreme love
living in expectant hope

———

Woven Through

God be in the fabric
of my life this day
Be sewn into
the hem of my garment
Be woven through
the wool
of words and work

Tribes

No culture can
contain you God
But no culture breathes
without you
You see all
hold all
love all
Creator God from every tribe be
praised

Reflection: Tribes

To Read: Acts 17:24-28
When human life was created, male and
female, it was described as being made "in
God's image". God's mark, the stamp of
his identity, is present somehow in his
human family.

When sin entered the world, the family fell
out. Abel and Cain feuded and subsequent
generations increased the fragmentation.
By the time Paul reached Athens the image
of God had been shattered into a million
different pieces. Cultures, language blocs,
tribes, families, ethnic groups - whichever
way you slice it, the human family is in tatters.

Yet Paul asserts that God is still head of
the family. He has watched over its
fragmentation. He journeys with each
branch and sets their boundaries, just as he
has journeyed with the Jews. Where is
God's image now? Contained in every tribe.
Complete in no one culture.

Week 34

monday

Idle Worship

Idols leave
their faithful
stripped and starving
God is fullness and freedom
Their love is emaciation
his emancipation

—◈—

tuesday

Outnumbered

When others
speak doubt into my faith
you are God
When questions
outnumber certainties
you are God
God my rock
be praised

Love vs Truth

Truth is a sword
Mercy is a healing balm
Show me God
when each is needed
Seeking love in truth
to speak the truth in love

—⁓—

Fashionista

If Christian, for you
is Dior
If gsus is just
a name for jeans
May the God who fashioned you
find you
Your designer become
your delight

Liminal

My day
is a threshold
on the brink
of possibility
or paralysis
Though the old
still stands
the new is always
waiting in the wings

———

Wisdom

We need wisdom
as a driver
needs fog lights
As a miner
needs a map
As a flight needs
a flight path
God of wisdom
lead us

G8

God is Gr8
In passion for the planet
In hope for the hungry
In anger at injustice
B4 the G8
even debate,
pray they C2
that God is Gr8

Reflection: G8

To Read: 1 Timothy 2:1-6
Paul's suggestion is not that those in
governmental authority are never wrong,
just that they have a God-given job to do.
Government is a calling - as much a
vocation as any other role. Our calling is to
pray for all who carry such a vocation.
That they might know God's wisdom.
That justice might triumph.
That peace might prevail.

Paul balances his call to prayer with the
bold assertion that only Christ can mediate
for us. Governments cannot save us. They
cannot bring us closer to God. Even the
most "godly" of political proposals will not
bridge the gap between God and men.
But those in authority have power to create
circumstances conducive to righteousness.
They have a responsibility to work for
peace. This alone is reason enough
to pray for them.

Week 35

monday

Reveal

As John on Patmos
I seek your inspiration, God
I cling to rock
and wait in rain
Bathe me in the light
that is invisible
but real

―∾―

tuesday

Crush Hour

Cappuccino
Café terrace
Evening traffic
Gentle sun
The city a ballet
of human movement
Move me, God, to your heart's beat

wednesday

Deeper

Deeper
than disaster
louder than loss
stronger than suffering
firmer than fear
Love runs
in the veins of God
and washes our world

—∞—

thursday

God Song

God sings to us
in the music
of what happens
The song that made us
Tones so deep
our ears don't hear
The melody of mercy

friday

Morning Prayer

Though the sun is risen
this road is in shadow
Warmth is coming
but we shiver
Come risen son
light our way

—❦—

saturday

Equation

We swim in the atoms
of the breath of God
We are spoken into being
imagined before we emerged
God thinking out loud = us

sunday

Bridges

Show me where
the bridges are God
between my world
and yours
May the peaceable kingdom
be a land I enter often
and know well

Reflection: Bridges

To Read: Matthew 7:7-11
C. S. Lewis built a wardrobe. Terebithia
was reached by a bridge. Never Never
Land lay beyond fairy dust, happy
thoughts and flight. Storybooks give us a
thousand ways of reaching secret worlds.

How do we cross into God's world?
How do the realities of heaven become as real
to us as the pavements we walk on? Jesus
gives us three answers. Keep knocking.
Keep asking. Keep seeking. This is about
prayer, but also about determination; about
focus, ambition and intention. You will see
God's kingdom when God's kingdom is
all you hunger for. When you thirst for it as
though crossing a desert.

"How can we know more of you, God?"
we ask. "How much do you want to?"
he replies. The answer we need, as so often,
is buried in his question.

Week 36

monday

Trust

When I worry
work on me to wait
If I ache with anxiety
embrace me
Where I'm frozen by fear
free me
God teach me to trust

—ᴠᴠ—

tuesday

Move Me

Move me God
from the battles
of my soul
to the ballet
of your wholeness
Draw me from my war
to your raw love

Warmed

And when the full son rises
we are warmed
Heat dries dew
light dismisses dark
We raise our faces
to the source of life

———

Fair Trade

To fear God
is wisdom
To be afraid of God
is a prison
Trade my terror
for tenderness, God
and my cowering
for confidence

friday

Turn

God of rescue and refuge
of shelter and strength
My still centre
My strong tower
When all is turning
may I turn to you

———

saturday

Chain

Christ be the chain
the binds you
Benedict said
The captivity
that completes you
May God
your guard and gate
ground you

Ruins

Where the ground
is dry, God, break out
in new springs
Where lives
are in ruins
restore
Where walls
are broken down
rebuild

Reflection: Ruins

To Read: Isaiah 58:9-12
The Exile gave Israel many new ways of
understanding God, many new images to
know him by. One of them is buried here,
at the climax of Isaiah's heartfelt cry for
justice. God is the one who rebuilds.

The picture is of the once glorious
Jerusalem: city of God and symbol of his
triumph. The city is in ruins, its walls
broken down. But the prophet foresees a
return to the City and to God. He speaks
of redemption and renewal, of a
rediscovery of God's ways, leading to a
revival of God's blessings. And he sees
rebuilding as a sign of that revival.

God is the one who restores, who renovates.
He specialises in bringing new
life to ruined places. Are there ruins in
your life? Can you dream of God's
rebuilding presence?

Week 37

monday

Breathe

As I breathe
without thinking
As I hunger
without trying
As I walk upright
without knowing how
So may I pray
without ceasing

—⟋⟍⟋—

tuesday

Slow

Slow me God
to contemplate
Reflecting
your reality
Receiving
your presence
Resting
in your sure
and certain hope

wednesday

Trouble Me

Trouble me God
where indolence lurks
Let the sword of your love
pierce my heart
Wake me
Break me
Remake me as your child

———

thursday

Prismatic

Radiate
your wisdom God
through the prism
of my life
May pure white light
become
your many colours
Make me a refraction
of you

Begin

I can't receive
what I don't ask for
I don't ask for
what I can't imagine
The pathways of prayer
begin in the imagination

—⁓—

God

God is the road I take
God the city it leads to
God waves me off
God waits to welcome me
God is my journey
God my goal

Graffiti

Graffiti your grace
on the walls of my life, God
Finger-paint
the words I need to see
Where warnings come
may I read well

Reflection: Graffiti

To Read: Daniel 5:1-6

Banksy has become one of Britain's most
successful artists. He is as widely known
as a painter can expect to be while living.
His works can sell for significant sums.
But his "canvas" remains the walls of the
world. He has graffitied in his home town
of Bristol, in London, New Orleans and
Bethlehem. And while some of his work is
whimsical, much of it carries a strong and
subversive message.

God, it seems, is capable of the same.
He interrupts Belshazzar's feast with a
devastating message-on-the-wall. The
meaning is not at first clear, but the intent
is unmistakable. The king quakes with fear.

Where might God write today, to get your
attention? What surfaces might he paint on?
Are you ready to receive and interpret
the messages he sends you?

Week 38

Stand

I stand among
the foolish
and the fallen
Grace alone
redeems me
God's love
not my performance
Frees me

———

Emoticon

Give me emotional wisdom, God
a gut-feel for what is right
and the guts to say and do it
May my heart feed my mind
and my mouth heed both

wednesday

Bookends

Like an unborn child
there is life
I have yet to see
Like a dying man
there is much
I regret already
Between womb and tomb
hold me God

———

thursday

Bend

When I bend
beyond belief
God, my God
is still God
When doubt is joy's jailer
and fear faith's thief
God, my God
is still God

Flawed

To be human
is to be flawed
Born bruised
redemption does not
start again from scratch
Redemption renders beautiful
our scratches

———

Waves

As waves wash
this coastline, God
Carried by currents
and worked up by the wind
So may your Spirit's ocean roar

Isaiah 60

Every day our creator
renews his creation
Every dawn
brings healing light
Every sunrise
is a taste of resurrection

Reflection: Isaiah 60

To Read: Isaiah 60:1-7 and 9-22
To the Hebrew mind, sunrise speaks of
God's faithfulness: the world daily
re-created; each new dawn a new Genesis.

Isaiah uses the sun's rising as a symbol of
God renewing his purposes for Israel.
The nation has been discouraged, tested,
chastised by God for her disobedience.
But he will renew his love for her. His
purposes will be re-established. As surely
as the new sun rises, hope will not die.

In language later used by the apostle John,
Isaiah looks to the day when we won't
need the sun any longer. When God
himself is our light, dawn will be
redundant. Until then, his sun will rise on
us each day. The message? God will keep
working until his work is done. He will be
faithful to the end.

Week 39

Brood

When chaos reigns
When darkness covers
the face of a formless earth
Brood over me God
Hover near me
Speak a new beginning

Ice and Sun

There are no icebergs
on the surface
of the sun
Snow is a no-show
So must fear's fist open
in the presence of perfect love

wednesday

Words

God's words to me
are poems to a lover's heart
music to a blind man's ears
whispers of direction
to a traveller at night

———

thursday

Overlap

Let me live God
in the overlap
of art and worship
In sensitive surrender
Where poetry-is-prophecy-is-prayer
Open to praise

Unfamiliar

On familiar roads
God walks with me
declaring all is new
On unfamiliar paths
he is there still
whispering,
"All will be well."

———

Ancient Future

Lead me to treasures
buried in my past, God
Woo me with wonders
stored up for my future
From passion to promise
Parent me

Bones

The bones of saints
are buried here
A layered library
of lives to learn from
Train my eyes to read, God
May my heart follow

Reflection: Bones

To Read: Genesis 50:25, Exodus 13:19
The practise of keeping the bones of saints
has largely died out in Europe, though
there remain a few places where the habit
persists. The story of Joseph's bones is
remarkable, because his request is fulfilled
400 years after his death. With his dying
breath he proclaims the certainty of God's
help for his people and the certainty is
held frozen, as dry as the bones
themselves, for 4 centuries.

Honouring the bones of dead saints may
be misguided. Praying to them surely must be.
But letting history speak, remembering the
promises of God, knowing his faithfulness
across the span of centuries - these
are practises worth keeping.

Are there past promises you have forgotten?
Are there dry bones in your life,
in your culture, that speak still of the
faithfulness of God?

Week 40

monday

Trade

The currency
of God's economy
is trust
I can't trade my achievements
or cash in my cleverness
but trust will buy me
everything I need

———

Not To Speak

tuesday

Teach me, God
how not to speak of you
When words
are too narrow
a canal to carry you
When meanings
are too lean
for the load

wednesday

Ice

If all the world
were treetops
prayer would be
the nest I rest in
Crafted chapel
Safe haven
Strong in storm
and wilds of winter

thursday

God is not Good

God is not good
he is goodness.
He is not loving
he is love.
Defy my definitions, God
Mould my meanings
to your majesty

If

If all the world
were ice and snow
prayer would be
the blade I'd skate on
A spade to cut and carve my igloo
My help
my home

—∿∿—

New for Old

Timeless God
time makes
your mercies mine
Old as yesterday's stories
Fresh as today's bread
New as tomorrow's dawn

Roads

I seek the road
less travelled, God
Let love outlaw laziness
Let service outsmart self
Outfit me
for the hard hike
into holiness

Reflection: Roads

To Read: Matthew 7:13-14
The New Testament has many "road" stories. The road through Samaria that brought Jesus into contact with the woman at the well. The road from Jerusalem to Jericho that gave another Samaritan the opportunity to love. The Emmaus road, scene of a moving resurrection conversation. Paul's road to Damascus, dramatically interrupted ... his journey was diverted, his purpose changed.

Every one of these stories involves choices: the choice to take that road in the first place; the choice to respond to what is found along the way. Each story results in dramatically changed lives.

Perhaps our faith is, in essence, all about roads and choices - the roads we take and the choices we make on them. May you choose, today, the road of loving service. And may the choices you make on it bring God glory.

Week 41

monday

Thread

For all my questions
in all my doubts
the life that shoots
like a thread
through the beauty of the world
sends me singing to my God

———

tuesday

Desert

If all the world
were desert
prayer would be
a cave to save me
Sheltered from sun
and windstorm
Alone, at home with my God

wednesday

Day

Day breaks trembling
with the taste of God
Time tingles
with his tender presence
God is the glow
at the edge of everything

—∿—

thursday

Bing Bling

Crooners sing
of falling in love
I hear God's mellow invitation
to fall into love
I let go
I trust
I fall
I land softly

Deep

As deep
as I have dug before
God is deeper
As wide
as I have wandered
God is wider
Holding my heart
God is my hope

———

Rock

As I hold this rock
God my rock grips me
As solid as this
small stone
in my hand
may his still Spirit
be my strong centre

Sweetness

Take the events
intended to harm me
Re-use them for good
Reframe every lost moment
Boil the bitter
into sweetness, God

Reflection: Sweetness

To Read: Judges 14:12-18

Samson's famous riddle was for years printed on the side of Golden Syrup tins. It is clever and entertaining. But it is also instructive. Perhaps, without knowing it, Samson was proclaiming God's intentions for his own life. He is strong - stronger than any man alive. Strength is his most obvious characteristic. But it is also his downfall. It makes him attractive to women and a soft target for their flattery. It leads him into violence. It saps his reliance on God.

And all the time God is trying to bring, out of Samson's strength, sweetness. It is obedience God wants, born of sensitivity and reliance and trust. A weaker man might have known that all along. But it takes Samson a lifetime to learn. Until, at last, he surrenders his strength to God's purposes.

Week 42

Loud

May strangers' needs
speak loud to me today
In blessing may I find
that I am blessed
In loving wide and well
may I win life

———∽∾∽———

Loved

Under a star-filled sky
I should feel small
Uncounted suns span
unmeasured miles
unaware of me
Why then, under this sky
do I feel loved?

Child

God in whom
all fatherhood is founded
teach me how to trust
God on whom
all motherhood is modelled
teach me to receive

—ɷ—

Fly

Through the bars
of my cage,
I see you, God
An eagle in flight
defining freedom
How can I come close to you?
Free me to fly

Wonder Full

God, the glory of the earth
is your glory
The splendour of the skies
is your splendour
The wonder of the stars is yours
wonderful creator

———

Establish in Me

Move in my imagination, God
Prefigure and pre-cook
your movement in the world
Establish in me
what your kingdom
can be through me

Noisy Us

You are found
in stillness, God
In silence
your voice rings clear
Still us
noisy as we are
to know you.

Reflection: Noisy Us

To Read: Isaiah 30:15
"In quietness and confidence shall be your
strength." These words sound a rare note
in a world in which noise and activity are
our security. We complain about being too
busy, but panic when the busyness ends.
We decry the noise of the world, but fear
silence more. We are annoyed by crowds
but afraid to be alone.

To learn to live with silence is a gift.
To find pockets of stillness in a noisy day is a
blessing. Confidence comes when you can
stand before God, naked, noiseless and
alone, and know that you are safe in his
wordless love; undone enough to re-enter
the noise of life renewed.

Will you allow God to still you?
Will you seek him in quietness and confidence?
Will you allow his silence to hold you secure?

Week 43

monday

Strong

In order to love
I must know myself loved
To serve I must learn
to be in need
In my weakness
loved by others
I am strong

—⁓—

tuesday

Race

God fired
the starting pistol
of the universe
God will hold
the finishing tape
of my life
The beginning and the end
is love

Enough

Teach me, God
the economics of enough
If in greed
I ask too much of you
If in fear
I ask too little
Measure to me daily
my bread

———∞———

Far and Near

Global, you glow
at the furthest frontier
Local, you love
to the deepest detail
Maker of mountains and microbes
be praised

Unhidden

Where truth is told
justice is possible
Where light shines
healing can flow
Naked before God
unhidden
we find
rest

—⚬⚬⚬—

Arc

Prayer is God's arc welding
Love leaping
Heaven earthed
Kingdom sparks
across the gap
between what is
and what can be

Grip

Hold me, God
in the grip of grace
Fold into me forgiveness
Free me
Keep me
Craft me
I know I'll grow
if you don't let go

Reflection: Grip

To Read: Romans 8:31-39

Ever worry you might lose your hold on God? Ever feel doubts rising and faith struggling to keep its footing? Ever feel that your grip is slipping? These are the times you need to know: God will never lose his grip on you.

The meaning of grace is that God holds you by his strength, not yours. Your role is to surrender, to accept his embrace, to know yourself as loved. It is God's grip on you, not yours on him, that gets you up the mountain.

The only force under heaven that can loosen God's grip on you ... is you. Like a child refusing love you can wriggle free and sulk in the corner. But if you will stop squirming, if you will allow yourself to be loved, he will hold you.

Week 44

Shine

The stars in chorus
deafen in their silence
Burning in cycles
a billion years long
Unquestioning
Obedient
So may I shine

———

Shores

I stand on
the shores of God
The sound
of pounding waves
Winds
from a distant shore
His depths
the ocean beyond

wednesday

Grate Full

If kindness is like cake
I've had a plateful
If blessings are beer
I have a crateful
Like a roaring coal fire
I am grateful

---

thursday

Farm

Where thorns encroach
and thistles threaten
God give me a
farmer's wisdom
To plant good seed
To make strong fences
To know
what to uproot

friday

River

In stillness I sense
the movement of God
In silence
I hear his footsteps
Below ground
under the surface
a river is flowing

—◈—

saturday

Pacing the Cage

In prayer
I pace the cage
of circumstance
I am cornered, captive
In God I see
a great savannah
stretched out before me

Compass

I move by modern maps
Recognised roads
Simple signs
You walk ancient ways
Deeper paths
Signs subtle to see
Guide me God

Reflection: Compass

To Read: Jeremiah 6:16
SatNavs have taught us to trust only the most recent maps. Online maps can change daily. With a programme even a few weeks out of date, we fear becoming lost. A principle of "newest is best" is invading our culture and "updating" is our new survival discipline.

The principle works well in satellite navigation, but may not be transferable. The Bible seems to suggest that there are ancient paths for us to seek and find - that old ways might, in the end, be more reliable. Are there ancient paths and practises hidden under the dust of your life? What might it take to rediscover them?

What disciplines of long ago might God re-ignite for you? What words and songs and prayers are waiting, now, to guide you? May you find, today, the ancient way.

Week 45

monday

Right Here, Right Now

In Amsterdam
I hear you say "I Am"
In the fields of France
I find you
Everywhere
is "here" to you God
Everywhen
is "now"

⸺✦⸺

tuesday

Repaint

Recolour my consciousness, God
Restore
Revive the vivid values
I once owned
Renew me
Repaint your planet
through me

wednesday

Foghorn

Mercy like a net
fine but strong
holds me
in the purposes of God
Faithfulness
like a foghorn
soft but clear
calls to me

—◦◦◦—

thursday

Space

Give me a silence, God
that's big enough
to meet you in
Carve a clearing
in my clutter
By your Spirit
shape a space

Signs

Signs are all around
Grace like a gritting truck
is spraying the streets
Resurrection
like a rumba
sounds out
the world's new rhythm

———

Sweep

As a pale sun
bathes this winter town
Your love God
warms my heart
As a fresh wind blows
to clean these streets
Spirit sweep my soul

13

Tongues of angels
Words of men
Soldier's sword
Poet's pen
Sounds on earth
Songs above
Nothing has meaning
without love

Reflection: 13

To Read: 1 Corinthians 13:1-13
These words are penned by Paul, widely
recognised - and sometimes criticised - as a
man more comfortable with creeds than
compassion; more known for dogma than
deeds of love. And yet these words speak
of a vision that subverts such an emphasis.
This is the anti-dogmatic, non-judgemental,
open and inclusive heart of a
gospel of mercy.

Religion? Paul spent the first half of his life
pursuing it. It almost killed him. In its
name he watched others killed. Grace, for
him, has been a liberation - a revolutionary
change; a second chance he knows he
didn't deserve. He is an addict freed of his
addiction, a sociopath healed of his
psychosis. Paul has found love to be the
centre of everything. Those who use him
to foster hate neither understand nor
honour him.

Week 46

Known

God is the ground
of my being
He numbers my neurons
He delights in the dance
of my DNA
I know above all else
I am known

―♒―

Root

In caverns
of your seadeep silence
God, may I learn to listen
In the soft heart of
your rainsoaked soil
may my soul take
root

wednesday

Layers

This is a city of layers
Life's traffic
holds the surface
Beneath it questions lie
Deeper still
the sounds
of God's new city
rise

---

thursday

Prod

From every detour
and distraction
I am dazzled by
disentangle me
Every wrong turn redeem
Patient Father
prod me homewards

Book

The world I walk in
is the book of God
The fire of his passion
infuses every page
In his presence
everything is illuminated

—◈—

Weather

Rain falls in sheets
across the coastline
A cold wind cleanses
So may my heart's landscape
be washed
by the Spirit's weather

Pillars of the Earth

Save me God
from shallow dreams
and small designs
I want to live my life
for beauty
Give me courage
to build a cathedral

Reflection: Pillars of the Earth

To Read:Proverbs 13:22
Few truly great works are completed in a
single generation. You might make an
important contribution. You may be a
crucial link in the chain: but it is unlikely
that anything that really matters will impact
you alone. The most important seeds you
plant may well not be harvested for
generations to come.

This is why "doing the right thing" can
never be measured by immediate, visible
results. Sometimes, the right thing makes
no sense in the moment. It may be years
after your death before the rightness of
your actions is seen. Think of Deitrich
Bonhoeffer. Think of Martin Luther King.
Neither lived to see growth from the seeds
they planted. But their children's children
eat the fruits still.

Don't build a hut for your own enjoyment.
Build a Cathedral for the generations
who follow.

Week 47

Unconfined

God of oceans
and open spaces
come dwell
in my small soul
God universal
and unconfined
make a home
in my heart

—✺—

Final Film

When the final film is shown
how will our ending appear?
As triumph
or as tragedy?
Daily we decide how
the human story ends

Glaze

Winter sun bathes buildings
Washes over walls
A pure clean light
An unexpected joy
So may grace glaze
the streets I walk

—∾—

Glocal God

Global God broaden
my vision
of your worldwide work
Local Lord deepen
my discernment
of your particular presence

friday

saturday

Hungry

Hungry I bring to you
my emptiness, God
Weary
I come in weakness
Bruised
I offer brokenness
Fill me, God
Free me
Fix me

—ⁿⁿ—

The Gift of Fire

When human tribes
walked in darkness
and feared
the noises of the night
God gave the gift of fire
Spirit fall in fire
on us today

Talent Show

Make me, God
a genius of generosity
Gracious in giving
Lavish in love
Give me the soul of a servant
and a heart to help

Reflection: Talent Show

To Read: Matthew 25:14-30
The chapter that brings us the tale of the
sheep and goats also speaks to us of
talents. What will you do, God asks us,
with the talents you have been given?
Will you use them to do good and bless
the poor?

One of the reasons the rich get richer and
the poor get poorer in our world is that
more talents are used for the former than
the latter. Geniuses of engineering make
new toys instead of new solutions. Brilliant
artists sell their gift to advertisers.
Entrepreneurs work for selfish gain instead
of altruistic achievement.

There are exceptions - brilliant, shining
examples of love and service. But there
aren't enough. What would happen if
every genius in the world turned their
talents to the plight of the poor?
What would happen if you did?

Week 48

monday

Midst

As a breeze blows
through the reeds
of the riverbank
God moves in our midst
As an eel in water
we move in the midst of God

———⁓⁓⁓———

Gift Shower

tuesday

God is a gift-giver
gregarious, generous
defaulting to grace
Salvation is
his gift-shower
Redemption is receiving

wednesday

Birthday

Years pass by
like road signs
We note the numbers
Celebrate in song
And every sign
also bears the words
"God is faithful"

———

thursday

Night Sight

Give us night vision, God
to see you in the dark
May we find in the shadows
the contours of your presence

friday

Remade

We are formed by
the Father
shaped by the Spirit
stretched by
the story of the Son
remade by our maker
to be marvellous

—⁘—

saturday

Old Friends

Sometimes
you are silent God
sometimes it's me
who has nothing to say
Thank you that friendship
doesn't always ask for words

Centre Me

Centre me, God
in the place
of your dwelling
Where kindness rules
and selfish hearts
can't enter
May I find
my home in love

Reflection: Centre Me

To Read: Daniel 6:10-12
We have enough of Daniel's story to know
that he was taken from Jerusalem as a
young man - probably still a teenager.
By Chapter 6, about to meet the lions, he is an
old man and has had a long and
distinguished career in the Babylonian
Civil Service.

Does he believe that he will one day see
Jerusalem again? Unlikely. The text
doesn't imply any such hope. Is he still
homesick? Also unlikely - his Babylon
years have outweighed his Jerusalem years
3 to 1.

He looks to Jerusalem because it is his
focus, reminding him of his identity and his
God. His residence is in Babylon, but his
centre is not. It is possible, Daniel shows
us, to live in exile and live well, by staying
centred on the presence and purposes
of God.

Week 49

Strike

As a sculptor knows
where to strike the stone
I need to know
my purpose in the world
Show me, God, the difference
you are asking me to make

—⁂—

Dross

As light to find
what otherwise was lost
come, Redeemer, come
As fire to burn
what otherwise
was dross
come, sent one of God

Risk

Incarnation is God's decision
to dive into the ocean
of humanity
Even at the risk
of drowning
may I learn
to dare
such love

—∾∾—

Paris

All the nations meet
in these streets
Rich and poor
Lovers and losers in life
The human family
God's love affair

Advent

In these moments
when our best selves
dare to dream
I pray
don't let these dreams
be wasted God
Let the good prove true

—∞—

Moments

In the frenzy of a frantic day
I shape a space called silence
Only moments long
but wider than the world
and deeper
God meet me here

Good

Though I wait long
to live my dreams
God means it for my good
Though adversity slow me
And barriers block
God means it for my good

Reflection: Good

To Read: Genesis 50:14-20
An epic tale of loss and redemption,
Joseph's story has as many rollercoaster
moments as a Hollywood blockbuster.
Its key is found here in Genesis 50:20.

A victim of vicious bullying and abuse at
the hands of his own brothers, torn from
his father, sold into slavery, falsely
accused and imprisoned, Joseph is able to
say in the end that, "God meant it for
good." God let it all happen, he asserts, so
that he would have the power to help his
brothers in their hour of need. The same
brothers who abused him.

This is total forgiveness, total trust in
God's care - a picture of grace centuries
before grace was talked about.
What circumstances do you face that might look
different if you could believe that God
meant them for good?

Week 50

Follow

Faith climbs the mountain
blindfolded
finds a path beyond sight
feels its way
Give me courage today
God to follow you by faith

—ഗ്ഗ—

Highway

Out of exile God
call me home
In alienation
forge vision
in isolation, hope
Send dreams until
I dream
a highway back to you

monday

tuesday

Trust

We swim under an ocean
of unfilled expectations
We want too much
Need too much
Take too much
Teach us, God
a simpler trust

———

Christmas Mass

Meet us, God
in this holy cave
of memory and song
Faltering faith
and fragile hope
flame into life this night

Christ Day

Meet us, God
as we celebrate the Christ Day
Midwinter exodus
Earth's re-creation
The day religion died
and hope was born

—◦◦◦—

Snow

Snow slows our world
deepens our sense of silence
Places our plans on hold
Calls us home
Snow, in its own way
is a Sabbath

Loopholes

If I've been looking for loopholes, God
may I look for love
If I am a lawyer
approaching the bench
may I be a child
in a father's embrace

Reflection: Loopholes

To Read: Luke 10:25-29

Comedian W. C. Fields is said to have reached for the Bible on his death-bed, breaking a lifetime's habit. When asked why, he said, "I'm looking for loopholes."

This religious expert is doing much the same thing. His goal is not to find out who *is* his neighbour, but who *is not*. Who can he situate outside the limits of his love? Jesus' answer - the story of the Good Samaritan - sets in place the kingdom principle: there are no loopholes.

How much of our legalistic codifying of religious practices is actually an attempt to find loopholes? We make detailed laws we can obey to divert attention from the ones we'd rather not. God didn't want our slavish obedience in the first place. He's sewn up all the loopholes to drive us towards love.

Week 51

Due Season

If things take time
let hope hold on
If solutions are slow
may I stay strong
Give me a farmer's faith, God
for fruit in due season

—⌇—

Currency

Rarer than rubies
Surer than soil
Greater than gold
Older than oil
Larger than life
Deeper than death
wisdom is the currency of God

Europe

Restore us, God
Where fields of faith
are overgrown with thorn
replant
What death and doubt destroy
may we rebuild

———✦———

Stone

Where I walk too slowly, God
give me courage
and a boot at my back
Where I run too fast
give me wisdom
and a stone in my shoe

friday

Eight Words

Eight words change
the course of history
Rebuild broken lives
Transform tragic stories
"I will arise
and go to my father."

—⚬⚬⚬—

saturday

Sludge

Deliver me, God
from the sludge
of procrastination
Drive decision
Invoke action
Puncture paralysis
Free my feet
to follow

Winter Hope

There is a tingling
in the winter air tonight
A dream stirs
Hope wakes
The scent of expectation
Restoring God
Come to us

Reflection: Winter Hope

To Read: Isaiah 9:1-7

There is a reason we celebrate Christmas
at mid-winter and why it means so much
to us. Approaching the year's end, in the
darkest season, hope could so very easily
run low. But something in our spirit says
it needn't.

In the fresh night air, under unnumbered
stars, something tells us hope is real.
We know our planet is deeply troubled.
We see pain and loss around us. We sense the
confusion suffering people feel. Yet deep
inside we know that all is not lost. We dare
to believe that somewhere in the universe,
beyond the very stars we see, there is a
force for love and good and redemption,
and a reason for hope.

The Bible has a name for this hope: the Messiah.
Deep in midwinter, we long for his coming.

Week 52

Imago Dei

We will not trash
what you call treasure
We will not despise
what you declare good
Teach us, God, to honour
the works
that bear your image

—◦◦◦—

B52

I know what a gun is for
and what rocket launchers do
I know what a bomb is
and a B52
But what is a god for?
For making
all things new

wednesday

Stop the Traffik

This day God
is eating chocolate
Savouring the flavour
Singing out the names
Of slaves unchained
It tastes of freedom
God is smiling

—∾∾—

thursday

Friends

In the night's deep silence
God be with you
Screen flickering
Room empty
Friendships of
140 characters
God be with you
Where you are

Father

Father of the fatherless
Embrace
all that is orphaned
within me
Lover of the loveless
Disperse
every trace of bitterness
you see

—◦◦◦—

Reflective

God make me
More reflective
than reactive
Instead of grabbing
may I give
Where self-congratulation
rears its head
bring self-control

Consider

To a lily God is Lagerfeld
To the birds, Raymond Blanc
To the grass he is Gaugin
Clothe us, God
Feed us
Colour our lives

Reflection: Consider

To Read: Matthew 6:24-34
This is a passage about beauty and colour,
about trust and ultimately about who God is.
Worry and anxiety stem from lack of trust.
And lack of trust grows from a
wrong image of God.

To correct this, Jesus points to the
faithfulness of God in creation. Even in the
colours of flowers there is generosity and
abundance. Would a mean-spirited God
make daffodils? Could a tight-fisted creator
come up with the duck-billed platypus?
Could a miser make a peacock?

God treats the non-human creation with
joyful abandon, throwing colours around
like Jackson Pollock. How much more will
he show love to you, his chosen envoys.

Don't follow a greyscale God. Take the
energy you've saved by not worrying and
plough it into getting to know the full-
colour version.

Last Word

Let love evolve
Let ego go
Oppression cease
And peace increase
Shelf self
Set pride aside
Embrace grace
Embrace grace
Embrace grace